3 8⁰⁰

A Taxi Driver's London

A TAXI DRIVER'S LONDON

by Maxwell Revenell Green
"THE CABBY WITH A CAMERA"

ARCO PUBLISHING COMPANY, INC.
New York

Published by ARCO PUBLISHING COMPANY, Inc.
219 Park Avenue South, New York, N.Y. 10003

Library of Congress Catalog Card Number 74-77365

Arco Book Number 668-01960-3

To *Ernie Propper for introducing me
to the Leica system*
To *Dennis L. Knowles for showing me
the technical application*

Printed in Great Britain

CONTENTS

Publisher's Introduction

Max Green is no ordinary taxi driver. I jumped into his cab, selected quite by chance, in Baker Street at 2.22 pm and somehow tumbled out at Paddington station in time to catch the 2.30 express to Newton Abbot, clutching in my hand a piece of paper with his name and address and with the fact in my mind that he had a unique collection of London photographs taken during his day's work which might be turned into a book. This is the book.

David St John Thomas

Introduction

Cabbing is one of the last of the individual jobs—there is no guv'nor watching over you, go where you like, stop when you like—with reservations of course, if you want to make money—you work according to your needs However, there is no end product for your work; a passenger is delivered from A to B and the job is finished, yet you have no sense of achievement. I have turned to photography as a creative outlet, using my cab as a mobile unit. In this way the two complement each other, for it is while driving my cab that I come across an unexpected situation, which may be pathetic, ridiculous, even tragic. Personally, I look for the humorous side and while I admire the tourist sights like Big Ben, and St Paul's, it is the everyday human happening that attracts me. This is what makes my job interesting. For this reason, and because I enjoy people and life, I am a 'day man' as opposed to a 'night man'.

In order to miss the main traffic, I usually leave home before daylight and 'mooch' along the Finchley Road in the hope of 'trapping' a job to town.

Very early morning work may more than likely involve market work. I enjoy the pace and I'm prepared to have boxes strapped all over the car—and I am also expected to waste frustrating time waiting for a street to clear, as this scene from Covent Garden shows.

A cabby's nightmare—these people move for no-one 'til *they* are ready!

Occasionally I get a call for a tour of London, and a little history on the side is useful. I like to take people to the Tate Gallery and ask them to compare Britannia with that on a penny. As these pictures show, the Tate Gallery Britannia is holding the trident in the wrong hand! When the sculptor saw his mistake, he was so upset that he committed suicide from the top of the parapet.

Mid-morning may find me at one of the northern stations to meet the incoming provincial trains. In this job one becomes a shrewd judge of character, and as soon as my fare approaches I can tell instinctively whether he is a 'regular', or a 'Connaught Ranger' (stranger), what district he is going to, what the tip will be! Not that I'm infallible—on one occasion I was called to a Chinese restaurant, where I was asked to join a funeral procession. I waited and was surprised to find that every car had filled except mine and that we were ready to go. I was then told I was for the spiritual ancestors! Out of curiosity I asked how many.

'Six' was the answer.

'Pity', I said, 'I'm only supposed to take four', so they called another cab for the other two.

For lunch I generally make for one of my regular eating places, Paddington Station, or the Marylebone Grill, which is a favourite haunt of drivers. Cabmen tend to be habitual creatures! We haunt the same ranks, eat at the same cafes and use the same shelters. We know each other by faces and numbers, very rarely by names, and amongst ourselves we tend to group into pre-war drivers and 'butterboys' (post war), radio and non-radio.

Lunch time line up outside the Marylebone Grill

Inside a cab shelter, a place to eat for cabmen exclusively

It's always interesting to pull on a rank, and meet a few old faces, and occasionally new ones. Things have changed even since I started driving in 1950. The pace is much faster now, the season more extended, but it's still possible to have a 'binder' (long wait) on a rank, and when ranks are filled this is a sure sign that things are quiet. During this time you get to hear of the working day of the other drivers, a 'morning job' when someone changes digs, usually at the weekend; two nuns loaded with fruit and vegetables from their morning's shopping at Covent Garden; a job ferrying a crippled person to and from hospital—shop talk which one only hears on the ranks, or in a cab shelter.

One of our drivers, who used to be a professional boxer, picked up two American servicemen, who asked him if he could get them a couple of young chicks. Because it was so late, the only place he could think of was a place called Barney's in the East End, which the men agreed to. Off they went, and the driver disappeared into Barney's. After what seemed an age he emerged triumphantly with two small neatly wrapped parcels.

Amazed, one American turned to the other 'Don't these guys understand English?', he said, as he outlined in the air the unmistakable curves of a woman.

Very few people realise just how much time and effort is spent by the apprentice cabby to gain his 'knowledge' of London. He must spend one-two years riding a bike (nowadays a motor-scooter) round approximately half a million streets, not to mention the inside points like hotels, stations, hospitals, clubs, museums, houses, shops. Nothing annoys me more than when a passenger tells me the exact route from A to B, then infers I am driving half-way round London to get him there. In fact, because of conditions within the trade, the sooner I can get rid of one passenger, the quicker I can pick up another, and the more profit I make.

A cabman has no basic wage or holiday pay—we are commissioned agents with tips, and I think a lot of bad feeling is created about the London cabby which could easily be avoided. When you take a cab, look at the clock, add your tip, and never be afraid to ask us questions—we're human, contrary to some people's belief! Never leave a taxi with a problem which might be sorted out. As an average guide to tipping, for a fare up to 5s say a tip of 1s; for a fare up to 10s, say a tip of 2s. Of course it's up to you, but if you think you have had good service, surely it's worth something extra?

13

The very name London Airport always seems to stir up (in my opinion undeservedly) heavy feelings between the riding public and the cabbies! I remember picking up a chap who wanted to go to London Airport. From the moment we started he was hopping up and down in the back, repeatedly telling me to go faster. I must have been chugging along at forty-three mph and considering the age of the cab that wasn't bad, so I told him 'Leave off. I'm going as fast as I can. Anyway, what time is your plane leaving?'

He told me it was the 1.30 to Paris.

'Oh, that's all right' I said, 'that plane is always late'.

'I know', said he wryly, 'I'm the pilot'.

The day's routes depend on prevailing conditions and seasons. The Motor Show in October would involve a lot of station and Earls Court district travelling. During the Chelsea Flower Show, I can run a ferry service between Victoria Station and Sloane Square. The pre-Christmas period causes chaos round the West End. Whereas I am looking for a fare on one hand, I am also on the lookout for a story on the other. If I have a fare aboard and I spot a crowd, I would avoid the congestion. But with an empty cab, I would follow it, camera at the ready. The crowds are there for something, and if it is round mid-day it may be a State visit.

(below) Judges en route from Westminster to the House of Lords prior to the Opening of Parliament

President de Gaulle and HRH the Duke of Edinburgh

The late President Kennedy

Royalty and accidents always draw large crowds! In the case of fire, you may even find a clearway prepared by the fire engines.

Another time I was flagged down by a very agitated woman, who was quite distraught, and asked to be taken to the nearest police station.
'Me Joey's been murdered' she cried.
I rushed her to the station and waited for her. She reappeared very shortly with an unamused sergeant who didn't want to waste his time on the death of her budgie!

My attitude to the job is the first hand I see I stop for, irres-
pective of who, where or when. Of course, with this attitude I
never know where I am going or where I will end up. On
one occasion at Notting Hill Gate an elderly woman waved
me down with a wreath.
'Quick, they've just gone', she gasped as she jumped in.
'Where?' was my obvious reply.
'To a cemetery somewhere near Ealing'. She hoped to catch
the procession at Shepherds Bush. As luck would have it we
caught up not with one but two processions at Shepherds
Bush, one going left and the other going right. My passenger
still could not give me any help as she had only known the
dead man. I decided to follow the procession to the left, until
it became obvious that this was not going near Ealing. We
doubled back and arrived just in time to join the second procession as it entered the cemetery.

17

I was let in for an awful lot of cracks from the lads when I
answered a radio call to go to a monastery to pick something
up for the BBC. On arrival at the monastery I found I was to
deliver an 'old habit'.

It is very hard to determine one's day—you have got to ride
with it. I usually try to avoid rush hours, which involve long
hours standing still in traffic, so at about four I head north
for home to make the changeover with my 'nightman', and
settle down to develop the day's pictures.

The morning rush hour at Charing Cross—note the happy
faces

(above) Built specially for a film, the *Bounty* at anchor in the Thames

(right) Boadicea strikes again!

A choirboys' outing—or a film sequence for television?

Meeting Point

As in any major city in the world, London is a meeting point for millions, and where people meet situations develop and the unexpected happens

(right and below) A change of circumstances brings a change of heart!

Trafalgar Square is a popular rendezvous and with a little spiritual assistance from the Bishop of Southwark one can rise above the crowds

Captive audience?

'I wonder if the beds are more comfortable inside?'

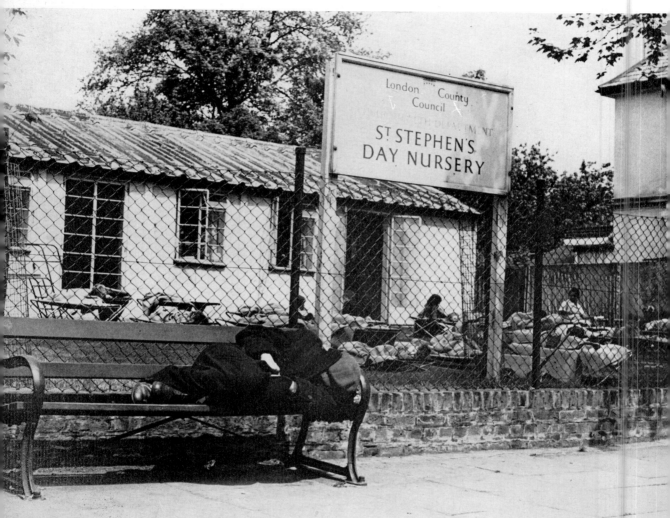

'Night Must Fall'

Military horses cooling off at Whitestone Pond, Hampstead.
A rare early morning scene caught before anyone else was
about—a cab and telephoto lens proved a most effective
camouflage

Another use for the pond when the roads become impossible!

Londoners turn out in full force for a State occasion. (opposite) A sombre crowd pays its last respects to Sir Winston Churchill as his funeral procession passes Ludgate Hill

(below) 'I've got a horse', famous saying of the late Prince Monolulu, 'a professional tipster' seen here during a visit to London

The Police at Work

An impressive line-up of law before Parliament

A duck and her family receive mounted police escort across the Mall—Royal treatment for a Royal Duck

In a normal day's work a policeman may be called upon to
lend a helping hand to keep things moving . . .

. . . or a restraining one!

The strong arm of the law!

Every day dead on time! A policeman clears traffic for Life Guards returning to Barracks

(opposite) Police cope calmly and smoothly with accidents, even when fate in the form of No 13 door seems to have had a hand in it (below)

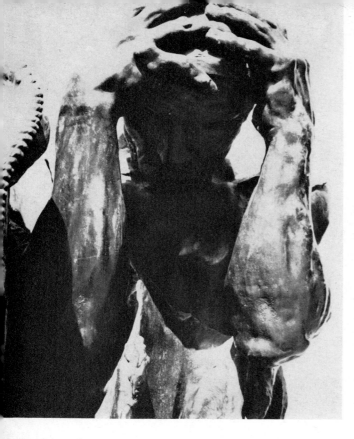

Art

It's all in the mind!

(left) Statue in the grounds of the Houses of Parliament

(below) Spring exhibition at Victoria embankment

Still life!

The elements combine with the work of man to create an exciting new art in Hyde Park

To appreciate a good painting one needs a good setting

(left) Curly the artist working at Hyde Park Corner. He specialises in 'Laughing Cavaliers', but since his pennies were repeatedly stolen he now prefers to be a nightwatchman.

(below) Working in the Chelsea district, an artist who prefers to live in the past—she specialises in Victorian art

'Daily Art' in Trafalgar Square

Although rapid advances are being made everyday in the design of cars, according to statistics the average time to get from A to B remains the same. (below) Horse and carriage in Hyde Park

Horse and Carriage

Old Plodder! A brewer's dray, an attractive sight to be seen around the city

'Totting' in Holland Park—an apprentice rag and bone
man learns the trade

The last of the 'low loaders'—a taxi which has seen many blooming days. A loader is an old cab—the type that had a collapsible roof and an open side beside the driver, and a little half door. During the war they used to tow fire tenders around

Pavement Workers

Unfortunately, it is becoming more and more rare to come across a scene such as the one below, which shows a knife grinder at work in Chelsea. Working in the open air—which makes the job very much a seasonal one—and lack of apprentices, contribute to making this a dying craft. They do not advertise for work, for their reputation is passed on by word of mouth. Note the ancient hand cart, which is pedal operated

(above and below) Mending chairs the old fashioned way

Replacing a lamp in Knightsbridge

The old lamplighter in Portland Place

(above) Trade for a shoe shine boy
in Piccadilly while another (below)
positions himself hopefully for the
rush hour at Charing Cross

Selling by example

Onion wallah!

Markets

'You want it, we've got it' can certainly be said of the London markets, which can compete with anywhere in the world in number and variety. The three largest and most well-known, Covent Garden, Smithfield and Billingsgate, are specialist markets for the trade only. The smaller markets for the public are supported enthusiastically by serious shoppers and casual buyers alike.

(below) early morning scene shows part of Covent Garden, the fruit, veg and flower market

West Smithfield meat market at Holborn
(above) A porter leaves his barrow unattended for a moment. It needs considerable strength to remove it—the barrow has solid iron fittings and fully loaded can weigh half a ton or more!

(below) Porters unloading

A porter at Billingsgate fish market, wearing the special leather hat on which to support the fish. The fish is auctioned from Customs House and is then distributed to the various destinations, generally arriving by 11 am. There is a charge of one penny per cwt of fish brought into the market

(above and facing page) Bermondsey market is frequented mostly by the dealers, many of whom resell the goods at a considerable profit the following day at the Portobello Road

Favourite hunting ground for a 'bargain' is the Portobello Road, home of antiques (above) and bric-brac and rubbish (opposite)—the fun is sorting out which is which

Club Row

Club Row—a Sunday morning market for animal lovers, where it is possible to buy any domestic pet from a hampster to a tame crocodile.
(below) Goldfish being inspected as they swim unconcernedly in their hanging polythene bags
(facing page top) A Great Dane hands over her family with some misgiving (below) The birds' stall is unfailingly popular

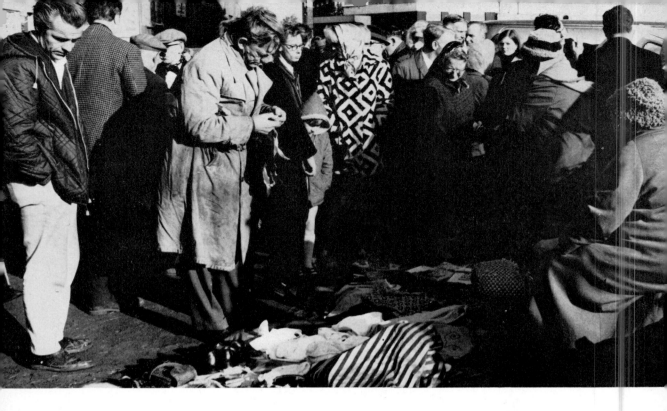

A little further up the road from Club Row, a customer tests
(above) and rejects (below) his find

Farringdon Road open-air book market for the literary-minded seeking manuscripts, old books, etc, provides competition for Charing Cross Road

Buskers

Many buskers are dedicated musicians who play for the love of music, but prefer to work in the open air . . .

(below) Harp in the North End Road

Others play from necessity

Bach in the Strand

Territories are strictly respected, although a group may hand over to another when finished for the evening

This group, the Road Stars, has entertained from Leicester
Square to Times Square, New York

Why should the Devil have the best tunes—or players!

Non stop dance act for Piccadilly shoppers, provided by the
'Earl of Mustard'; originally he was part of a double act
called Mick and Mike, who used to play a barrel organ. When
one died, the Earl of Mustard carried on alone. He changes
his act as often as the weather

Modern pied pipers in town, attracting their own queue.
Dick Charlesworth and his City Gents—a very famous jazz
band

Changing Patterns

Generations apart, but together they lean on their tools!
Redevelopment at Hyde Park Corner

Three stages of progress on the Barbican site

'Heart of Oak' crumbles

Contrast in the city. Modern development meets part of the old London wall

Cleaning in the city. (left) Wash and brush up for Nelson in Trafalgar Square

(below) The cleaning of St Pauls whispering dome takes several years

(below and opposite) A three dimensional view of work in progress adjoining the site of the Temple of Mithras, with St Pauls in the background. Note the top of the scaffolding tower which appears in both pictures

Bureaucratic notices in the city

The Tudor Gateway to St Bartholomews Church, Smithfield.
This is the oldest surviving church in London which until
1915 was covered with bricks and mortar. The lovely
beamed facade was revealed as the result of a bomb

Characters

In my job I come across thousands of people I shall never see again —others I see all the time, according to the situation or the district I am in. They are not famous, but they are 'cabby's characters'.

(left) Old Soldier—Old Sweat

(below) Paul, famous pub pianist from Marylebone—his unconventional dress serves him summer and winter

My favourite captain . . .

. . steers his course through Camden Town

(facing page and below) Birds and characters tend to encourage each other, guarding their relationship and territories jealously

(above and facing page) Pearly Kings and Queens collecting for charity are a familiar scene in London. The elaborate and traditional costumes are carefully handed down from family to family

You might glimpse this recluse very early in the morning during a weekend in the city—but not if she sees you first

Lavender lady in Victoria

Annual Events

One of the events closest to my heart is the Norwood Annual outing, when 60-70 cabs take 350 under-privileged children to the coast for the day.

(opposite above) Anyone under the wheels?

(below) Ready for take off

From adventure to reminiscences! Chelsea Pensioners preparing for their day's outing to Worthing, which usually takes place in June

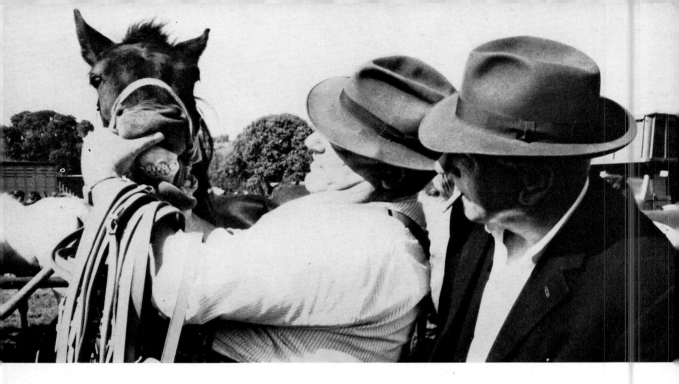

'Ye Barnet Horse Fair' the only horse fair in the south of England is held at High Barnet. All deals are settled by word of mouth and a clap of the hand—nothing is ever written down.
(above) Buyer makes a thorough inspection before concluding his deal (below)

Every convenience

Entertainers come into their own in the various side-shows. This scene shows the raw egg eater, whose winning total consumption on this occasion was 38 raw eggs

Once a year, a familiar domestic scene which is taking place all over England is also to be seen in the Parks of London, as the leaves are gathered and burnt

On the occasion of the Queen's birthday, Hyde Park becomes the scene of the Charge of the Light Brigade

Barge traffic on the Thames comes to a halt for the
yacht race

6 November Trafalgar Square; the morning after the explosive
night before

Time

Perhaps the most significant clock to any Londoner is St Mary-le-Bow, better known as 'Bow Bells'. Anyone born within the sound of the bells is a cockney. Rebuilt by Wren—devastated in 1941 when the Tower was burnt out—dates back to 1090

St Dunstans, Fleet Street.
This clock was made in 1671, then pulled down from this site and bought by the Marquess of Hertford for £200 to put in his home in Regents Park. He then gave it to St Dunstans for the Blind. Lord Rothermere bought the clock from the School and in 1935 it was returned to its original site in Fleet Street

This beautiful sun dial was broken up when the Russell Hotel was pulled down

98

Swinging London—time for advertising in Piccadilly Circus

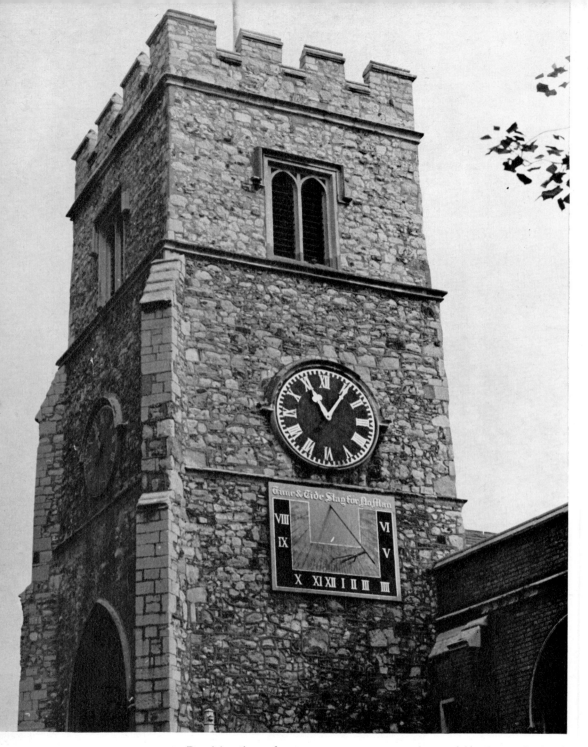

Double time for prayer, an unusual combination of clock face and sundial is shown here on the tower of Putney Parish Church

Time for the connoisseur—the
ornate green, cream and gilt clock
above Fortnam & Mason, Piccadilly

Liberty's Arch, overlooking Kingley
Street, W1

Knightsbridge Barracks
Another clock which was eventually demolished with the rest of the building

(left) this beautiful archway was taken down piece by piece and reassembled elsewhere by a private buyer

102

Time for politics
'Big Ben' at Westminster, the most widely heard of all clocks

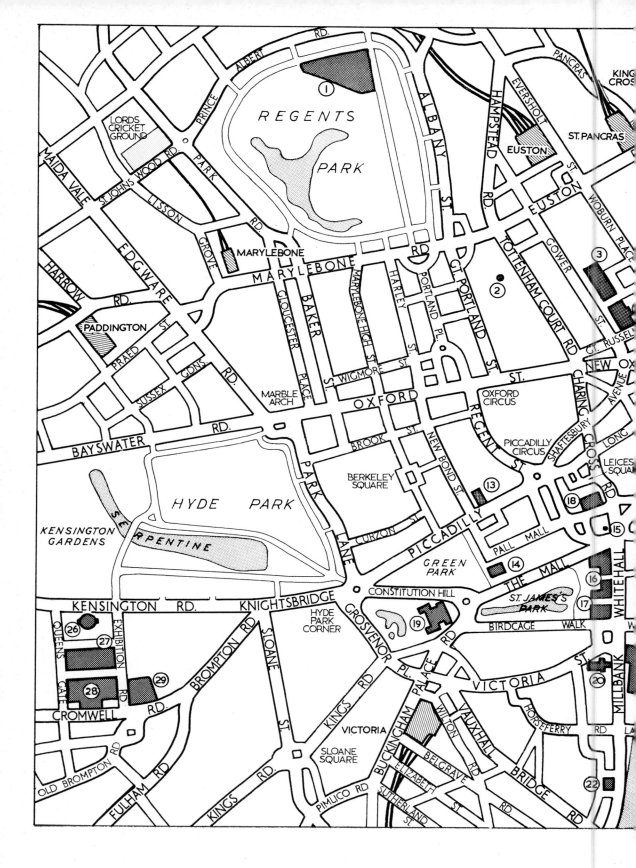

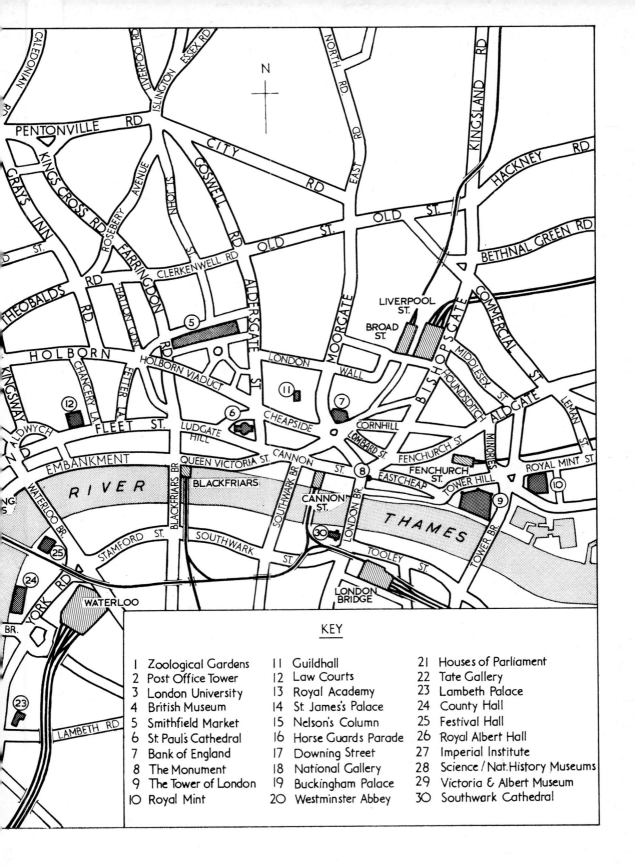

KEY

1 Zoological Gardens	11 Guildhall	21 Houses of Parliament
2 Post Office Tower	12 Law Courts	22 Tate Gallery
3 London University	13 Royal Academy	23 Lambeth Palace
4 British Museum	14 St. James's Palace	24 County Hall
5 Smithfield Market	15 Nelson's Column	25 Festival Hall
6 St. Paul's Cathedral	16 Horse Guards Parade	26 Royal Albert Hall
7 Bank of England	17 Downing Street	27 Imperial Institute
8 The Monument	18 National Gallery	28 Science / Nat. History Museums
9 The Tower of London	19 Buckingham Palace	29 Victoria & Albert Museum
10 Royal Mint	20 Westminster Abbey	30 Southwark Cathedral

Time for law
Law Courts in the Strand

Canon St

Clerkenwell and Harlesdon, both
subscribed by public donation

St Georges overlooks the three boroughs which subscribed towards the clock. The black face of the clock overlooks the fourth and non-subscribing borough!

Time to celebrate
Christmas time at Selfridges, Oxford Street

Time for a drink—fitting advertisement for Henekey in the form of a barrel

(above) Early autumn morning in Hyde Park
(opposite) London by night—the Houses of Parliament and
the Royal Festival Hall